Richard J. Daley

In Memory

Edited by James L. Spurlock
Designed by Donald J. Spurlock

Manol Publications Ltd.

Photograph and illustration credits

Cover and title page photographs: *Chicago Tribune*

Archdiocese of Chicago: 132 (top and bottom); Better Government Association: 138 (top); Chicago Park District /Frank Nocita: 104; *Chicago Tribune*: 11, 13, 14-15, 19, 22, 27, 33 (bottom), 38, 49, 55 (top and bottom), 75 (bottom), 79, 80, 81, 82 (top and bottom), 83 (top), 84 (top), 86, 103, 109, 110, 112, 113, 117, 118, 120, 121 (top), 123 (top and bottom), 124, 125 (top and bottom), 128, 141; Frank Held: 32 (bottom), 72 (top and bottom), 73, 74 (top and bottom), 75 (top); Ray Hillstrom: 119) top), 122; Jerry Kupcinet: 5; Ken Niimi: 144; Frank Nocita: 105; Stanley Tretick: 136 (bottom); UPI/Compix: 29 (bottom), 30, 41, 42, 45 (bottom), 52 (bottom), 53 (top and bottom), 59, 62 (top), 83 (bottom), 85 (top), 94 (top), 95, 99, 102; Wide World: 21, 23, 29 (top), 31 (top and bottom), 33 (top right), 33 (top left), 37, 40, 43 (top and bottom), 44 (top), 50, 51, 52 (top), 54, 61 (top), 62 (bottom), 63, 64 (top and bottom), 65, 69, 70, 71, 85 (bottom), 87, 91, 92, 93 (top and bottom), 94 (bottom), 100, 101, 111, 119 (bottom), 121 (bottom), 129, 133 (top and bottom), 134 (top and bottom), 143 (top and bottom).

Library of Congress Catalog Card Number: 77-126
ISBN Number: 0-918516-01-3

First printing February 1977

Printed in the United States of America

Manol Publications Ltd., 676 N. LaSalle St., Chicago, Illinois 60610

Table of Contents

A "Consummate Man"

by Edward V. Hanrahan

Some commentary following the death of Mayor Daley proves Shakespeare was right in saying the good that men do "is oft interred with their bones."

Richard J. Daley may not have been a saint. However, Chicago, and every politician who took him as an example to follow, are immeasurably better because he was so much more than a "powerful machine politician," as he was called.

Unfortunately, because of political differences, I was on the outs with Mayor Daley the last few years. Nevertheless, I knew him well before that. And fairness compels me to correct false impressions given of him.

Mayor Daley loved Chicago far more than most of his critics did. He worked harder than most of them, every day trying, in his way, to make it better. Sure, he could have done more for the neighborhoods than downtown. Yet the physical conditions of most Chicago neighborhoods and the essential city services Chicagoans get (police, fire, refuse collection, street and alley lighting, parks) are far better than those of New York, Philadelphia, Cleveland, Detroit.

The Mayor was always linked to the 1968 Democratic Convention, which many Chicagoans remember with distaste, sadness and regret. Those confrontations didn't bring out the best in him, the protest movement, our city or the news media. Neither side can honestly be defended. Yet those incidents were no more representative of Chicago — or Mayor Daley — than Kent State was of Ohio and its people, or Attica was of New York and Governor Rockefeller.

Moreover, those who stridently decry the events at that convention are never heard to lament the fact that the "silent majority" was turned off — and its awakening was put off — by the violence and vulgarity of the protesters.

Some have charged that Mayor Daley was out of touch with the times. Indeed, recent election losses (by other Democrats) have raised questions about his reading of the public mind. Yet there are few political leaders in this country with his record of victories, and no mayor of his national fame.

He understood Chicago voters so well that he swamped his latest mayoral opponents despite the many solid issues against him. He probably could have been re-elected as long as he wanted to run. What would Mayor Beame give for that kind of support from New Yorkers?

One of the reasons for Mayor Daley's automatic re-elections was that he and the Democratic organization had given countless persons city jobs. Those job-holders do provide neighborhood "intelligence" but, more important, they look after the people in their precincts so well they're generally considered members of the family.

In Chicago, garbage cans are "free," parking tickets may be "taken care of" and usually someone in need is helped by the Democratic organization. Maybe none of that's what the Founding Fathers had in mind, but if Lockheed can get a Federal loan of millions, if giant corporations caught cheating consumers can escape punishment by entering consent agreements, and if ambassadorships can be sold for Presidential campaign contributions, no wonder the average Chicagoan doesn't consider it unreasonable to ask for a "favor" every now and then.

Not surprisingly, his severest critics completely missed Mayor Daley's greatest accomplishment, the impact of his personal honest and exemplary family life upon every Chicagoan. His public and private life centered upon the traditional values of home, religion and friends. No family in the city had more devoted parents than Mayor and Mrs. Daley. None had children more respectful and less pretentious than his. His friendly word or "hello, dear" was freely given to everyone. Eagerly sought in society drawing rooms and corporate board rooms, he was at home in every neighborhood of Chicago and with every age group, though he publicly prided himself on being a senior citizen.

Many persons had political opinions and preferences different from his. Some even feared and disliked him for his politics, but it would be hard to find many who didn't respect him. He earned the esteem and affection of those who knew him because of how he acted, not who he was. His superior ability, character and hard work would have assured his success in any field. That he achieved it in politics, with an unscathed reputation for personal integrity, made him unique.

It's a pity that some persons were so disaffected by his image as The Boss that they didn't recognize him as a consummate man. For all other Chicagoans — and for thousands elsewhere — his death represents an irreplaceable, personal loss.

Edward V. Hanrahan, a Chicago attorney, opposed Richard J. Daley in the 1975 Democratic Party primary election for mayor.

Eulogy

by Irv Kupcinet

This has been an unusual week in Chicago. A co-mingling of joy and sorrow—joy over the Christmas holiday—sorrow over the death of Mayor Richard Joseph Daley: born May 15, 1902; died December 20, 1976.

Much has been reported about Daley in the press, on TV and radio — much of it accurate, but too much of it so gushy as to lose credibility.

Richard J. Daley was a mortal man, which means he had his faults and failures as well as his successes and spectaculars. In his case there were many more positives than negatives. His massive contributions to Chicago during his 21 years as Mayor need no repetition here.

He was, as we reported in our column, one of the most public of all public figures because of his long tenure in office. Yet he was one of the most private of persons, with only a handful of intimate cronies who had access to his private life.

His most cherished moments were in the confines of his home, with his wife Eleanor, surrounded by their four sons and three daughters and their grandchildren. This was the home-loving, private Richard J. Daley.

The public Richard J. Daley was the consummate politician who perhaps understood people and their ambitions better than any other political figure on the scene. His regard for the man on the street — the average person — was reflected by the tens of thousands of them who stood in line for hours to pay final homage to him when death came. This, to me, was more impressive than the attendance of such VIPs as President-elect Jimmy Carter, Vice-President Nelson Rockefeller and the Senators and Congressmen who assembled.

His regard for people was brought home to me one day in his office in City Hall. An aide came in to report on what he called the "derelicts on West Madison Street."

Daley immediately corrected him. "Don't ever call them derelicts," he scolded. "They're human beings and they will be treated as human beings."

He was called the last of the big-city bosses — and perhaps that was true — but there was a tendency in the media, and around the nation, to exaggerate his power.

That he had considerable power and, for the most part, used it for what he considered the good of Chicago, few can deny.

That he played hard-ball politics, none can deny.

But the essential point is that Daley knew the limits of power, what could be accomplished and what would have to wait for another day. The fact is that he was a master of the art of persuasion and he accomplished more that way than by a show of force.

And he was a man of decision. Once he reached a conclusion, he didn't hesitate to act, unlike so many other politicians.

I've seen and known Richard J. Daley down through the years. I've seen him in his worst moments, the 1968 Democratic convention, with memories never to be forgotten, and I've seen him at his finest moments — when he created excitement and electricity in the art of government with memories ever to be treasured.

History will record his rightful place, but we can say, by way of tribute:
THERE ... WAS A MAN.

Remarks

by Judge Abraham Lincoln Marovitz, Senior Judge, U. S. District Court

One somber December afternoon, that familiar smile that could take the edge off the coldest Chicago winter wind was gone; that impish leprechaun grin, as broad as the County Cork and as wide as the City of Chicago, was absent; that hearty rich laugh, which roared up from resources so deep and traditions so ancient that adversity and antagonism could not obscure it, was silenced. And while that laughter still echoes in our ears, that warmth still radiates in the chambers of our hearts, and that smile is forever indelibly imprinted on our collective memories, it is heavy silence that still hangs like a shroud over this city, though over a month has passed since Richard J. Daley's departure.

It is a silence born not from a paucity for praise but rather from an overabundance of accolade generated by decades, and indeed generations, of public service. There is so much to say, and how often do we wish now that we again had the opportunity to say it — to his face. But it is too late for that now, as is often the case with a great man, whose sudden loss is unfortunately the only thing that can jolt us into the realization of how much we have gained from him.

Yes, there are words that I, and I'm sure each and every person in this room, would have liked to say to Dick Daley in his lifetime. But now, 35 days after the people of Chicago and many of us in this room lost one of our dearest and most devoted friends, still numbed by intense sorrow, still stunned by profound grief, we are here to offer that always meager substitute: words of memorial, words of posthumous tribute.

It is very difficult to put into words a tribute to Mayor Daley's leadership and talents, when so much of what surrounds us stands as a more eloquent tribute. Much in the words of the inscription chiseled over the entrance of Old St. Paul's Cathedral in London, one of Sir Christopher Wren's masterpieces: "IF THOU SEEKEST HIS MONUMENT, LOOK AROUND." We have in our great city a Loop as prosperous as ever, with blueprints extending into the 21st century; the best public transportation system in the nation; a lakefront and skyline unmatched anywhere in the nation; the best illuminated and cleanest streets on the metropolitan scene; colleges beginning and universities expanding; progressive programs for the elderly; Youth Foundation educational scholarships; youth sports programs; and so much more. All of this growth and achievement is due in no small part to the efforts and inspirational dreams of Richard Daley.

With no disrespect intended, Your Eminence Cardinal Cody (ed. note: also a speaker at this luncheon), Dick Daley had two religions. Surely he was devoted to the Church, and attended Mass every day. But his second religion was Chicago. The City was also his cathedral, and just as surely he attended to the masses in that regard. It was precisely this devotion and enthusiasm that set him apart from other mayors, and enabled him to govern more effectively and truly lead his city. He worked harder, longer, more intensely, more enthusiastically and more zealously than any other mayor in the country. And through his tireless and dedicated efforts, Chicago has become known as a big city that is livable and vibrant — a city that works. In fact, last year at the Annual Conference of Mayors, Dick Daley was unanimously voted America's outstanding mayor. And just the other day, after his death, America's mayors paid tribute to him again at their 1977 Annual Conference.

But perhaps one of the most important aspects of Richard Daley's 21-year tenure as Mayor of Chicago was his appreciation and understanding that the overall development of a city should not be at the cost of its smaller neighborhoods. He realized that while a city must be greater than the sum total of all of its parts, it is the uniqueness of its parts that gives the city its flavor and character.

Richard Daley was the consummate public servant. He was a lawyer and he never forgot it. He had but one client — the City of Chicago. His tenure as Mayor was not unlike a long complex trial, and always he pressed the case of his clients, the citizens of Chicago, before State and Federal agencies. His brief for the City of Chicago was always ready; and he expended great amounts of energy appealing for the benefit of his constituents. He had his reversals, but like all good lawyers he won more often than he lost. He spent every working hour in his client's behalf, and the only fee he ever sought was the appreciation of his constituents, and the knowledge that his efforts were instrumental in making Chicago a better place in which to live.

And the people of Chicago appreciated his efforts, electing him six times as their Mayor. The relationship between Dick Daley and his city reminds me of a quotation attributed to my namesake, Abraham Lincoln: "I like to see a man proud of the place in which he lives. I like to see a man live so that his place will be proud of him." I believe I gave Mayor Daley a plaque with that quotation, which he kept in his office.

The love affair between Chicago and Mayor Daley did not die on December 20, 1976. It lives on, and will continue to live, for many of us, for as long as we reap the inspiration of his friendship, his guidance and his leadership.

For 21 years, Richard J. Daley was the City of Chicago. His name and his city were synonymous terms, inseparably intertwined the world over. For many throughout the country, in this city and in this room, it is difficult to distinguish between Daley the man and Daley the Mayor; between Daley the Mayor and the City of Chicago. And so, for many, unable to differentiate between the city and the man, there remains a mystery regarding the true nature of Richard J. Daley.

People still ask of what stuff was he made; they still wonder what compulsion drove him to devote such a great part of his life to a city and to public service; and they are intrigued by his rise to political prominence and his amazing control over the workings of each and every aspect of a complex and powerful political organization and city government. These are proper questions, particularly for those citizens of Chicago who until late last month knew of no other leader in their city — and for whom the immediate word associated with "mayor" was "Daley," and with Daley, "Mayor."

But cities are only bricks and mortar, and I want to talk to you about a man. I do not profess to have all of the answers to questions about Dick Daley, nor do I really think that anyone does. But I thought that if I could share with you this afternoon some of my feelings about a man I loved and admired, perhaps some light could be shed upon a man I was proud to call my friend.

What of the more private Richard Daley? The devoted husband, the proud father and father-in-law and grandfather, the dedicated and loyal friend and the man of great religious faith. Dick Daley had the rare ability to keep his private life private despite the great attention focused upon his everyday activities.

It was my privilege to be counted among Dick Daley's close friends for about 40 years, and his friendship is one that I will always cherish. How easily and freely some use the word "friend" these days, and how difficult it becomes to use such a common word for such a special friend, and such a very special friendship.

I think back to our years together in the Illinois State Senate beginning in 1939 when we were called the "Young Turks" — a strange name for a Jew and an Irishman. I recall that even then Dick Daley was a "mover," with a keen interest in social reform. Long before civil rights and social equality were popular, he joined with me in supporting a Fair Employment Practices Act and a Fair Housing Act. He had grown up in his own kind of tight-knit neighborhood, had enjoyed the beauty and cheer of a warm family life, and strived at every level of his public service career to help guarantee those benefits and pleasures to those less fortunate than he.

When we would visit, the first part of our conversation would invariably focus upon our families. He would tell me about his and ask about mine. We shared in each other's griefs and celebrated together in our joys. Our friendship was bottomed on a strong mutual respect that allowed for difference of opinion and constructive criticism — and we had our differences, on issues and people. And contrary to what some say or write, Dick Daley was receptive to constructive criticism, though he was intolerant of gratuitous negativism or contrariness motivated by purely partisan politics. He respected the loyal opposition, when that opposition was grounded in sincere disagreement. He was a man of few words, but when he spoke on any matter of public concern he was sure that he had done his homework, and expected anyone who opposed his position to be equally well prepared and ready to offer some viable alternative, for that was his practice. I recall that during our days in the State Senate, whenever Daley opposed a bill he was always prepared with a substitute bill which he sincerely believed to be more effective.

In the State Senate, and during his tenure as Mayor, Dick Daley gained a national reputation as an authority on municipal and state government finance. The mere fact that he was able to keep Chicago from deficit spending during the term of his leadership attests to his financial expertise.

Dick Daley certainly was an ambitious man, as most people should be — especially those who reach a high station in life. But the story of his life could hardly be labeled Blind Ambition. There is no question in my mind that he could have advanced politically well beyond the position of Mayor of Chicago. But to become the Mayor had been his ambition, and he believed in that position he could best serve the people. This is indeed the true test of a great man — the ability to assess where he can accomplish the greatest good, and not to permit himself to be enticed away by prospects of greater glory but lesser accomplishment. And so, rather than strive for higher office, he preferred to groom others for it. He became one of the most powerful voices in national Democratic politics. Yes, he wanted that power — but not for power's sake alone. Rather, he wanted it for purposes of fulfilling his dreams, for the greater good of his city, and his people.

During most of our private meetings, I never heard him talk ill of other people, even those who spoke or wrote disparagingly about him. He had a great forgiving spirit, inspired by his religion, and I would venture to say that he had the most oft-turned cheek of anyone I know.

At times he was disappointed and made truly heartsick by those whom he had helped and who subsequently misused their positions. But he was not a man to cast aside lightly or forsake years of friendship because an individual had erred. He truly believed that to err is human, and to forgive divine, and that justice should be tempered with mercy. Some say he was forgiving to a fault, but it is hard to fault a man for being a true friend. For he was — as I remain — part of an era in which family and friendships are holy bonds that are not easily broken, and are relationships that are built to weather the worst of storms.

We would often sit and reminisce about "the old days," telling stories about our respective neighborhoods and the characters who filled our days of youth. For Dick Daley, the past was not something to be forgotten. He felt that lessons could be learned from the past, and therefore throughout his public service life he remembered his humble origins, he remembered his people — and above all he remembered his family. There was rarely a conversation in the course of which his beloved dad Mike and mother Lil were not mentioned with love, affection and gratitude.

I would like to take a moment to say a few words about Mrs. Richard Daley. She too has been my dear friend. And while the late Mayor had a great romance with the City and the City with him, there was no greater love in the man than for the wonderful woman he affectionately called "Sis" for over 40 years. Sis was the one he wanted to please most of all, and she was the great inspiration in his life. She was the one upon whose strength and good sense he relied so heavily. She too was the one who played such a vital role in raising their fine sons and daughters who are so devoted to their parents and to each other.

Dick Daley was father and friend to his children. He took them all in his confidence and they in turn took him into theirs. They enjoyed a unique relationship. So too it was for those of his friends he took to his bosom. I for one will forever cherish the privilege of saying that Dick Daley was my friend, and for his friends may I say:

Once in a while a friend is found
Who is a friend right from the start;
Once in a while a friendhsip is made
That really warms the heart.
Once in a while a friendship is formed
To last the whole life through;
It really does happen — once in a while
And it happened to me and many of you here,
with our friend Dick Daley.

Dick Daley, in his lifetime, and after his death, was judged by many. But after all is said and done, there is that one Supreme Court to which we are all, one day, held accountable, that does the ultimate judging. Dick Daley is standing in front of that Court now. He has made his case and made it well. The Court, I am confident, has taken into account the millions of amicus briefs written in the hearts of the multitudes he helped, and who sorely miss him now. And I can almost hear that Court rendering its final verdict. "Richard Joseph Daley, your performance for Chicago and mankind is unanimously affirmed."

Let us continue in the spirit of that affirmance to do what we can, as lawyers and as citizens, for the City we live in, which City Dick Daley so loved.

From a speech delivered at Chicago Bar Association Commemorative Luncheon Tribute for Mayor Daley, January 25, 1977.

ANOTHER
BRIDGEPORT
BOY

Another Bridgeport Boy

Bridgeport, an area of Chicago just east and north of the fabled stock yards, has long been a neighborhood of close-knit, working class families — as well as a neighborhood that historically has produced an unusually high proportion of Chicago politicians. Bridgeport people often stay in the neighborhood throughout their lives, too, and Chicago's Mayor Daley was no exception.

Richard J. Daley was born at 3602 S. Lowe Avenue, less than one city block distant from the house at 3536 S. Lowe in which he would later raise his own family. The only child of Michael and Lillian Daley, he was recalled by friends and neighbors alike as a shy, quiet child. Perhaps this was because his father, a sheetmetal worker, was the same kind of man.

Throughout their lives, Daley had a very close relationship with his parents. Partly because he was their only child, they were able to spend more money — and more time — on his upbringing than was characteristic of most Bridgeport families. Daley was probably the "best-dressed kid in the neighborhood," and probably the only kid who always carried a clean handkerchief. (It is also said that when provoked, he was a good fighter.)

Lillian Daley was politically active, an unusual thing for a Bridgeport mother. She gave her son an early breath of the heady air of politics, sometimes taking him along when she went to political meetings. Always, she was determined that her son become "someone," and, because the family could

A young Richard J. Daley poses at a picnic (opposite).

afford it, Richard Daley went to De La Salle Institute to take commercial courses after graduation from the Nativity of Our Lord parochial school in 1913. The school was — and still is — located only a couple of miles away but in a neighborhood Bridgeporters hated and feared. Daley always went to and from school with a group of Bridgeport boys.

No one Richard Daley knew at De La Salle remembered him as obviously destined for greatness. But just about everyone he knew, from childhood on, remembered him as "affable," as someone who "could handle himself," as someone who had the talent of "keeping his mouth shut" when the situation warranted. All these talents were to stand him in good stead in his political life.

Graduation day; the Mayor attended college, and later law school at De Paul University, at night (above).

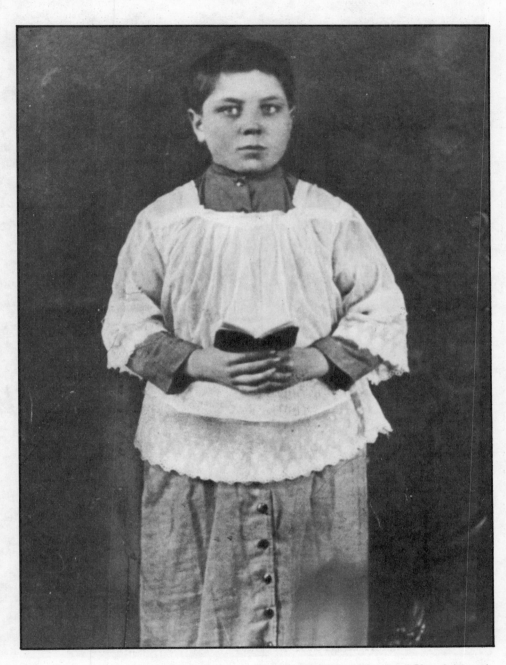

The Mayor was an altar boy at the Nativity of Our Lord Church (above).

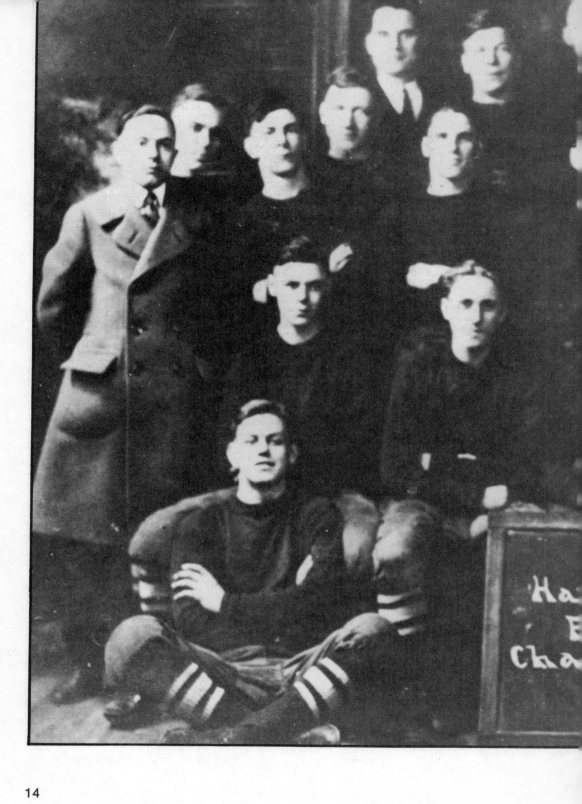

Twenty-one-year-old Richard Daley is third from right in the top row (arrow) in this 1923 photograph.

15

THE STOCK YARDS COWBOY THROWS HIS HAT INTO THE POLITICAL RING

The Stock Yards Cowboy Throws His Hat Into The Political Ring

The main key to Richard J. Daley's success as a politician was that he was a *grind*. He was like that fellow who everybody had in one of their school classes, the one who got good grades not out of extreme brilliance but by sheer hard work. He was willing to be just behind another fellow who was on the way up, willing to do the other fellow's work if need be, just as long as he got the other guy's slot after he was gone.

Daley got his start in the Hamburg Athletic Club, a Bridgeport organization that has produced more powerful politicians than any of Chicago's socially elite clubs. At age 22, in 1924, Daley was elected president of the Club, and he held that post for 15 years.

The importance of the Hamburg Club as a starting point for young Bridgeport political hopefuls is well illustrated in an incident described by Morgan Finley, clerk of the circuit court. Finley had returned from the Navy in 1946 and made an unsuccessful attempt to join the Club. "Daley was always ready to give you advice if you asked him, so I walked the block from the club and rang his doorbell," said Finley. "He put on his coat and went back with me to the Club and I was accepted." Later Daley gave Finley his start in politics by making him secretary of the 11th Ward.

Finley was following the same route taken by Daley, who had worked his way through law school at night at the same time he was beginning his career. Daley

Campaigning at Chicago's Union Stock Yards in 1955, Daley joins the Stock Yards cowboys on horseback (opposite). Daley himself had been a Stock Yards cowboy for a brief period over three decades earlier.

first became a public employee as a clerk in the City Council. He later served 13 years as Cook County deputy comptroller, two years as state representative and eight years as a state senator. He also served a term as state director of revenue under the late Gov. Adlai E. Stevenson. His real power base, though, came when Cook County Democrats elected him chairman of their Central Committee in 1953.

Two years later, he beat incumbent Democratic Mayor Martin H. Kennelly and Benjamin Adamowski in a three-way primary race. He then went on to defeat easily the Republican candidate, 5th Ward Alderman Robert E. Merriam. His victory count, 708,222, became his license plate number for the rest of his life.

It was a long climb to the top Chicago politics for Richard J. Daley. But to some who knew him early in his political career, there had never been any doubt that he would make it. One of Daley's fellow legislators was quoted as saying, "When other guys were out fooling around at night, Daley took home files of work, and he brought it back at least half and most times all finished."

The Daleys go to the polls in 1953, during the Mayor's tenure as chairman of the Cook County Democratic Central Committee (above).

Daley smiles confidently in this February 16, 1955, photograph. Six days later, the primary election would bring him his first nomination as Democratic candidate for mayor (opposite).

Mayor Martin H. Kennelly's concession to Daley in the 1955 primary election was cause for smiles all around (above).

Accompanied by Morris B. Sachs (left) and John C. Marcin, also candidates for city office, Daley leaves Democratic headquarters after a March 14, 1955, meeting (opposite).

MAYOR **DALEY**

Mayor Daley

Perhaps the main reason that Chicago became known as "the city that works" is that being Mayor of Chicago was the ultimate professional target for Richard J. Daley. After he won the office in 1955 at age 52, he considered that Chicago became *his*. If something about it didn't meet his muster, the buck stopped with the king of clout.

Though Daley's philosophy that "good politics is good government" rankled some, the Mayor figured you could knock his system but you couldn't argue with its success.

Success in Chicago is measured in nuts and bolts and, if some criticized his social consciousness, none could deny that Daley certainly was a master builder. Expenditures for construction, private and public, averaged $400 million a year under his administration and there were $300 million worth of urban renewal projects, a $2 billion expressway network and a sewage system that is one of the best in the world. There was O'Hare Airport, some of the country's tallest buildings and other construction galore. The Mayor's proudest achievement in building was the University of Illinois Chicago Circle Campus, on Chicago's Near West Side. He had a warm spot in his heart as well for the Civic Center and the beautiful Picasso statue on its plaza.

It takes more than construction to develop a reputation as the "city that works" and Daley's administration provided Chicago with something that many

Mayor Daley looks out over the Chicago City Council from his customary place at the podium (opposite).

big cities sometimes have to do without — service. Chicago citizens came to take for granted clean and well-illuminated streets, having the garbage picked up regularly and having police and fire departments that were envied by other urban forces.

One of Daley's greatest strengths was as a negotiator and mediator between municipal laborers and their employers. No other mayor could have believably delivered this pep talk to striking sanitation workers: "You men, with the help of God, are going to make this the finest city. You are going to go out and make every street and every alley the finest street and the finest alley."

That statement and others like it could only have come from Mayor Daley, and a Republican politician explained it as follows: "He considers Chicago *his* city. The sidewalks are *his* living room. The parks are *his* backyard. He just doesn't want anyone to screw it up."

Daley waves to the camera after casting his ballot in the April 1955 Democratic primary (above). Incumbent mayor Martin H. Kennelly had originally been nominated for Mayor the preceding February, but when he broke with the Democratic organization, Daley became the new nominee.

A smiling Dick and Sis Daley leave the 1955 Democratic primary polling place (right).

Daley makes his acceptance speech at his first mayoral inauguration on April 21, 1955. To his far right are his wife and four of their children.

Family and well-wishers applaud Mayor Daley after he captured about 70 percent of the vote in the 1971 mayoral election (opposite). His opponent in that election was Richard Friedman.

As he did in 1955, 1959, 1963, and 1967, U.S. District Court Judge Abraham Lincoln Marovitz (right) administers the oath of office in 1971 to Mayor Daley as the Mayor begins his fifth term (above).

On April 19, 1975, the day before he began his 20th year as Mayor of Chicago, Richard J. Daley posed in his office for this picture (left).

31

Rev. Jesse Jackson, National President of Operation PUSH (People United to Save Humanity), explains the "black power" handshake to Mayor Daley at the opening breakfast of Black Expo, which is sponsored by Operation PUSH, September 28, 1971 (left).

Mayor Daley speaks to a group of striking electrical workers at an outdoor rally, July 27, 1968, telling them, "I'm with you against anyone in Chicago" (right). The strike, against Illinois Bell Telephone Company, had threatened to remove the Democratic National Convention from Chicago until it was agreed that volunteer workers could install communications equipment in the International Ampitheatre.

Mayor Daley was instrumental in bringing the famous Picasso sculpture to the Civic Center Plaza (left).

Mayor Daley looks on as President John F. Kennedy lays a wreath on a monument to Lieutenant Commander Edward (Butch) O'Hare at the dedication ceremonies for O'Hare Airport, March 23, 1963. (above). The wreath was handed to the President by Philip Tobrea III (right, in uniform) and Edward Palmer, both relatives of O'Hare.

During topping-out ceremonies at the O'Hare International Tower Hotel on June 14, 1972, Mayor Daley relaxes for a moment and adjusts his hard hat (above). At Daley's left is Cook County Board President George Dunne.

O'Hare International Airport, the world's busiest airport, is one of Richard Daley's major achievements as Mayor.

NATIONAL
POWER

A National Power

At perhaps the pinnacle of his national power Richard J. Daley made a statement that was often recalled by the late President John F. Kennedy. Over cocktails, Kennedy related the story to Ben Bradlee (then *Newsweek* Washington bureau chief, now editor of the *Washington Post*). As Illinois electoral votes and the 1960 Presidential election hung in the balance, a concerned Kennedy phoned Chicago's Mayor. "Mr. President," said Daley (according to Bradlee's quotation of Kennedy), "with a little bit of luck and the help of a few close friends, you're going to carry Illinois."

There were accusations of vote fraud and talk of a contested election. But knowledgable politicos, including the inner circle of Kennedy's opponent, Richard M. Nixon, concluded that any questionable practices by the Democrats in Cook County were balanced by similar actions by the Republicans in southern Illinois.

Daley and John Kennedy's father, the late Joseph P., had planned the election of an Irish Catholic President for some time, frequently meeting for lunch in a private office of the elder Kennedy's Merchandise Mart, and victory was not to be denied.

"At no time, in the many elections that Daley had run since the first one in 1954, had the Democratic ward bosses been subjected to the pressure he applied for Jack Kennedy," recalls commentator Len O'Connor in his book *Clout*.

O'Connor also says that the second part of Daley's strategy, aside from producing a large vote, was to get the impressive tally recorded quickly. This was to discourage Republican voters in the western states. The ploy succeeded. While the western polls were still open, the television networks were conceding Kennedy a

Mayor Daley smiles and scratches his brow as Presidential candidate Jimmy Carter opens
his arms to greet a crowd at the Democratic State Convention on Chicago's North Side,
September 9, 1976.

massive Illinois victory and there was a noticeable drop in California voting near the close.

A personal sacrifice had also been made by Daley to achieve Kennedy's victory. He was offered the 1960 Illinois gubernatorial nomination, but he said: "I

Mayor Daley greets a young Sen. John F. Kennedy when the latter came to Chicago to make a speech, 1956 (below). Kennedy visits Chicago during his 1960 Presidential campaign (opposite).

President John F. Kennedy gets a typical Chicago welcome as his motorcade moves through the downtown streets (above).

Senator Edward (Ted) Kennedy chats with the Mayor during a fund-raising dinner for the Democratic Party, May 24, 1972 (below).

At the 1961 U.S. Conference of Mayors, Mayor Daley looks on as Vice-President Lyndon B. Johnson greets New York mayor Robert Wagner (above). Below left: President Johnson hands one of the pens he used to sign the Housing and Urban Renewal bill to Mayor Daley, August 10, 1965.

(Left) Governor Buford Ellington of Tennessee bends over to chat with the Mayor at the 1968 Democratic National Convention held in Chicago. Two conventions later (below) in New York, the Mayor discusses strategy with members of the Illinois delegation.

Mayor Daley and former President Harry Truman swap talk at a Springfield, Illinois Democratic fund raising dinner (above). The Mayor had just been named "best dressed man of the year" in 1969, so visiting former Vice-President Hubert Humphrey — grinning — feels the material of the Mayor's suit (below).

George McGovern smiles as Mayor Daley introduces him on August 24, 1972, as "the next President of the United States," after their first meeting since the Democratic National Convention earlier that summer (above).

Mayor Daley accompanies First Lady Pat Nixon as the 1972 Columbus Day parade steps off down State Street, Chicago's traditional parade route (above). Behind the Mayor and Mrs. Nixon are Rep. Roman Pucinski (left) and Sen. Charles Percy.

Mayor John Lindsay of New York joins Mayor Daley for a private conversation in Chicago, November 18, 1971 (right).

didn't think you could have an Irish Catholic for President and one for governor, too."

Daley's dream presidency was ended tragically with the assassination of John F. Kennedy. Though Kennedy's death affected Daley deeply, the Mayor quickly established a working relationship with the new president, Lyndon B. Johnson. Johnson respected Daley and invited him to be present at his first address in his new office.

"He's the best political brain in the country," asserted Johnson. "When I need to know about politics in the big northern cities and states, I telephone Dick Daley in Chicago and find out."

During his term at the helm of Chicago, Daley obtained federal funds to build O'Hare International Airport and billions of dollars for other public works, including new sewers and street lights and major improvements to the city's rapid transit system. Even under Republican Presidents Nixon and Gerald Ford, Daley continued to have considerable clout. The federal cash flow to Chicago was steady.

Though Daley later found himself having a tougher time on the national level and was unable to carry Illinois for Jimmy Carter, Carter did not forget what Daley had done for the party for over 20 years, and he flew into Chicago to attend the Mayor's funeral.

The morning the results had become obvious in the 1976 elections, Daley was questioned about the outcome by a woman reporter.

"Dear, you never look back," he said. "Tomorrow is another day."

HE WALKED
WITH KINGS AND
QUEENS . . .

He Walked With Kings And Queens . . .

Astronauts, missionaries, entertainers, kings and queens — they all came to Chicago for an audience with Richard J. Daley. It was a "feather in the cap" for a celebrity to have the opportunity to meet Mayor Daley while in Chicago. The famous from throughout the world always put Chicago and a visit with Daley on their American itinerary.

One of Daley's and Chicago's most notable guests was Queen Elizabeth II of Britain. Her visit provided Leon M. Despres, former 5th Ward Alderman, with one of his favorite memories of Mayor Daley.

"In the summer of 1959," Despres recalled, "Queen Elizabeth and the Prince Consort visited Chicago. As an alderman, I too was invited with my wife to the civic royal dinner. At the appropriate moment, music sounded, the doors of the grand ballroom of the Conrad Hilton Hotel opened, and Daley, with the Queen of England on his arm, entered and walked slowly to the podium and the main banquet table. What a sight it was to witness a poor Irish immigrant's son, now the head of Chicago's government, walking with the Queen of England to offer a civic banquet given by him! Daley achieved many triumphs of a more substantial nature, but none was more splendiferous."

Sometimes, though, Daley — for one reason or another — would make himself unavailable to a visiting notable. In 1976, for instance, Bobby Vinton and the head of a European royal family were both coming to town at the same time. Daley was expected at O'Hare Airport to meet the incoming king — but, as often, he did

Mayor Daley escorts Queen Elizabeth to a civic banquet at the Conrad Hilton Hotel (opposite).

48

things *his* way. The Mayor not only attended Bobby Vinton's concert, he later made him an honorary Chicagoan. The king would just have to wait.

While the adults enjoy the scene, sons and daughters of Mayor Daley move into position to have their picture taken with Queen Elizabeth II and Prince Philip at a reception for the visiting royal couple on July 6, 1959 (below).

Mayor Daley and other dignitaries greet Queen Elizabeth II and Prince Philip at a reception at Soldier Field (opposite). Behind the Mayor from left to right are Gov. William G. Stratton, Canadian Prime Minister John Diefenbaker and Wiley Buchanan, Jr., U.S. protocol chief.

Prince Bertil of Sweden enjoys a chuckle as he places the Royal Order of Vasa on Mayor Daley during a ceremony held at the Mayor's office, November 22, 1965 (left). Earlier, the Mayor had presented the City of Chicago Flag to the Prince.

Belgium's King Badouin comes to Chicago in 1959 and Mayor Daley meets the royal visitor at the airport. Several hundred high-school girls (not shown) were also on hand to greet the king.

An honor guard stands at attention as part of the welcoming ceremony for visiting Mexican president Adolfo Lopez Mateos in 1965.

Daley honors Apollo 13 astronauts John L. Swigert (center) and James A. Lovell (right) in an outdoor Civic Center gathering, 1970.

The Mayor shares a joke with Frank Sinatra (above).

Jack Benny presents the City of Hope plaque to Mayor Daley, January 13, 1957 (right).

The Rev. Martin Luther King, Jr., shakes hands with Mayor Daley on a visit to the Mayor's office with Rev. Ralph Abernathy, May 27, 1963 (opposite).

...AND AMONG THE PEOPLE

...And Among The People

Perhaps the relationship between Mayor Richard J. Daley and his admiring, working-class constituency was best expressed by a man who knew the Mayor all his life. "Richard J. Daley was a common person, and don't ever forget it," said Jimmy Barrett. "He treated kings and queens the same as he did a guy like me from Canaryville. That's why I liked the guy. The press always showed him as Daley the politician. They never showed him as Daley the man. I knew him as the man — who never let the office stand in the way of his feelings."

The Mayor pushed through all sorts of parks and recreational facilities for the people and at times it seemed there was a parade every day in Chicago, but it was his assistance to a neighbor that typified the way the Mayor lived his life. Fred Bedore, who had played handball with the Mayor in the Hamburg Athletic Club and lived two blocks from him for 68 years, lost his job and got throat cancer. He wouldn't ask for assistance, but the Mayor insisted and, for 16 years, the police and fire department's alarm office has employed Bedore.

It would be easy to explain away Bedore's case by noting that he was a neighbor. But that would be overlooking numerous other instances of the Mayor's feeling for his people. One example is the time a young couple unknown to the Mayor came to his office saying that they didn't have the fee for a marriage license. The Mayor paid the fee from his own pocket.

The Mayor's concern also extended to Chicago's city employees.

"I remember getting calls on my car radio to come to Bridgeport at 4 A.M.," said Fire Commissioner Robert J. Quinn. "Every time one of my boys was killed,

Carrying the traditional Irish shillelagh, Mayor Daley and honored guests march in the 1971 St. Patrick's Day Parade down Chicago's State Street (opposite).

58

I would get a call from the Mayor and he would invite me over to see him. So I'd go over and we'd sit down over a cup of coffee in his kitchen and I'd have to explain the death to him. I had to explain how it happened and how we could avoid such a tragedy in the future. He had this deep concern.''

Not a complex man, Richard J. Daley once tried to explain his relationship with Chicago and its people and found he could only express it in the most basic of terms: "I've been Mayor for 19 years. I would have to have a type of love to keep moving on. I do love Chicago and its people.''

Mayor and Mrs. Daley review the 1976 St. Patrick's Day Parade (left).

When Chicago's 34-mile-long Bike Route along the lakefront was dedicated on May 25, 1971, Mayor Daley joined in the spirit of the day by accompanying Keith Kingsbury, activities chairman of the League of American Wheelmen, on a bicycle-built-for-two (opposite). At right is Florence Gibson, 75, a retired schoolteacher who bicycles seven miles a day.

The "Mayor Daley Girls" kick high during a rally for their candidate at Chicago's famed Aragon Ballroom on March 29, 1971 (right). More than 5,000 people from five North Side wards jammed the ballroom to cheer the Mayor, who was seeking his fifth term.

Mayor Daley, carrying an American flag, heads a "freedom march" down State Street by the National Association for the Advancement of Colored People as part of Chicago's 1963 Independence Day celebration (opposite). At the far left is Charles Evers, walking hand in hand with the son Darrell, 10, and daughter Rena, 8, of his late brother, NAACP field secretary Medgar Evers.

Arriving for a speaking engagement just before the 1975 primary elections, Mayor Daley shakes hands with Conrad Hilton Hotel doorman Ted Tomazak (below).

Mayor Daley dons a sombrero and meets with a group of his Spanish-speaking constituents during the 1975 campaign for the mayoral nomination (above). Embracing him is Martha Garcia.

HE
NEVER
LEFT
BRIDGEPORT

He Never Left Bridgeport

Immediately after Richard J. Daley was elected to his first term as Chicago's Mayor in 1955, a rumor spread that he was going to move out of Bridgeport. This was after the Mayor had described himself during his campaign as the "son of a Chicago working man . . . reared in a working class community . . . who played on the sandlots in the great stock yards, worked in the stock yards and dreamed . . ."

The rumor was quickly quashed when Sis Daley made this public statement: "We wouldn't dream of moving. We love Bridgeport."

"I was born in this neighborhood and I still live in it," said the Mayor many years later. "It is a stock yard area but they're good, honest people, they're hardworking, they have large families with modest incomes."

The Mayor continued to reside in Bridgeport and a change did come to the neighborhood of small houses and apartment buildings where Irish, Lithuanian, Italian, Polish, and German people resided. More and more members of the community came to have political jobs, though the exact count was always a closely held secret.

In private life, the Mayor preferred the company of his neighbors to that of the powerful and influential people he encountered in public life. Bridgeport residents were invited into his home, where many more powerful individuals had never been. "I went to a lot of parties at his house, like his grandson's graduation party," said 16-year-old Katie Cernok of 3649 S. Union. "They just got together and sang Irish songs and he never acted like a big shot."

The Mayor, like most people in the neighborhood, would sometimes stop for a glass of beer at Schaller's Pump or have a sundae at David's Restaurant on S.

On his 67th birthday in 1969, Mayor Daley stops to greet young Matt Danaher, Jr., before leaving for his office. His limousine's license plate bears the number of votes cast for him the first time he became Mayor, in 1955 (opposite).

Halsted Street. "He was a once-in-a-lifetime friend," said Jack Schaller.

Bridgeport residents returned the Mayor's love, demonstrating their affection at every opportunity, especially when he was under criticism. The sentiment they showed during the 1968 Democratic National Convention was a perfect example.

"Acting like a big shot" was never Richard J. Daley's style. When his oldest son, Richard M., was elected to the 1970 Illinois state constitutional convention, the Mayor broke down during a formal speech and said: "I hope and pray to God when he's on the floor of the convention he'll always remember the people from whence he comes and that he'll always fight for the people."

Mayor Daley's neighbors rally around him as he prepares to return to his office (above) after spending several days in seclusion during the 1972 Democratic National Convention. His delegation had been refused seats at the Convention.

70

Much controversy arose over the Mayor's use of police and National Guard troops during the 1968 Democratic National Convention. But his neighbors continued to support him (above).

This Chicago Police Department precinct oversees Bridgeport, the Chicago neighborhood in which Richard J. Daley lived his entire life.

This house (above) is the headquarters of Bridgeport's Hamburg Athletic Club. Young Richard Daley joined this club in the 1920s; it was the starting point for his long political career.

One of Mayor Daley's earliest paid political jobs was as secretary of the 11th Ward Regular Democratic Organization.

Mayor Daley was born in this building at 3602 S. Lowe Avenue (above).

Shortly after Richard Daley and Eleanor "Sis" Guilfoyle were married in 1936, they built this house at 3536 S. Lowe (above) and the Mayor lived in it for the rest of his life. As their children were born, additions were built on the back of the house.

Mayor Daley worshipped at the Nativity of Our Lord Roman Catholic Church throughout his life, and it was there that thousands of Chicagoans went to pay their respects to his memory on December 21 and 22, 1976 (right).

Above: The 3500 block of S. Lowe Avenue is quiet and still in the days following the Mayor's funeral. The Daleys' home is second from right.

A FAMILY MAN

A
Family
Man

Marrying Eleanor "Sis" Guilfoyle was the greatest event in his life, Richard J. Daley often said. And, despite all his power and prestige, Daley was foremost a father and husband.

Daley recalled his first impression of Sis: "She certainly was a fine Irish girl."

Lloyd Guilfoyle, an acquaintance from the nearby Canaryville neighborhood, introduced his 19-year-old sister to Daley at a Hamburg Athletic Club softball game. Daley was playing second base. A paint-company secretary, petite, blonde Sis was known in the area for her beauty, and her strict Catholic upbringing was compatible with Daley's.

Daley was neither a "lady's man" nor did he possess the Irish gift of gab. It was four years before the two began dating seriously and then Daley courted Sis for two more years before they were married.

When they returned from a two-week honeymoon, taken in the midst of Daley's first political campaign (for state representative), Sis was carrying their first child. Yet she continued as his first and favorite campaign manager.

Daley won that first election and even though his political star continued to rise, the happy couple never left their little pink Bridgeport bungalow. They merely added more rooms as more children were born. After a hectic day, Daley would return by limousine to his South Lowe Avenue home and, often, a meat-and-potatoes dinner with some of Sis' home-baked Irish soda bread.

Sis did not want a mayoral mansion. She said: "We never wanted to disrupt our children's lives or schooling by moving into an official mayoral residence."

Richard and Sis Daley leave the church on their wedding day in the summer of 1936 (opposite).

The children continued to be the center of Daley's personal life. When he first won the mayoral race in 1955, he shut down victory festivities shortly after 10 P.M. to take his children home to bed.

Daley was a loving but firm father. "I've always urged the children to speak up," he said. "Of course, I always spoke last."

He recorded the childhood of his seven children on reels of film shot with a weathered Bell & Howell. Later, he took snapshots of his grandchildren with a Polaroid SX-70.

Through the years, the family's personal life was kept private at Sis' request. She stayed out of the limelight and kept her opinions to herself — with rare exceptions.

"Once he comes home he closes that door and ceases being mayor," she asserted.

Daley's close friend Patrick O'Malley, president of Canteen Corporation and one of the few family intimates, recalled: "He loved that family like nobody, I think, and no father ever loved a family more."

On the Daleys' 35th wedding anniversary, Sis said: "He was my first and only love. I dearly wish we could have 35 more years together.

The Daley children add elaborate decorations to their 1951 Halloween pumpkins as their proud father looks on (below). From left are Eleanor, Richard, Patricia, John, William, Michael and Mary Carol.

Father and son (Michael) return from a shopping trip in 1955 (opposite).

A proud Sis Daley shows off the bronzed baby shoes of some of her children (above).

The Daley family accompanies their husband and father to the polls to vote in the 1955 primary elections (above). John holds his father's hand; Eleanor is at Sis Daley's right; from front to rear, the children at Sis' left are William, Michael, Richard and Mary Carol.

The family poses for a portrait just after the elections of 1955 in the new Mayor's City Hall office (above). From left: William, Michael, John, Richard, the Mayor, Mrs. Daley, the Mayor's father Michael, Mary Carol and Eleanor.

The musical comedy <u>Oklahoma!</u> was presented at the McVickers Theatre in the mid-1950s and Mayor and Mrs. Daley brought the family to opening night (above).

The proud father escorts his daughter Patricia into the church for her wedding, 1966 (left).

Michael Daley sits in a limousine with his bride, the former Barbara Lynn Paterson, November 18, 1972 (below).

The new Mr. and Mrs. John Daley make their way through a crowd of reporters and photographers outside the Nativity of Our Lord Church, May 28, 1975 (above). She is the former Mary Lou Briatta.

Sis Daley prepares to film son Richard's entrance into the Illinois Senate as the Mayor talks with Richard (left) and Richard's wife (back to camera) (above).

The Mayor, his wife and two of their sons head for the polling place to vote in the 1972 elections (above). Behind the family are two plainclothes policemen.

Mayor Daley relaxes at his Grand Beach, Michigan, summer home in August 1974 while recuperating from surgery performed the previous June (above). The Mayor and his family vacationed at this retreat on the shores of Lake Michigan whenever the Mayor's busy time schedule permitted.

A DEVOUTLY RELIGIOUS MAN

A Devoutly Religious Man

The morning did not begin officially for Richard J. Daley until after mass. Every working day he would depart for church at an early hour, kissing his wife Sis on the cheek and striding out to the limousine parked and waiting in front of his bungalow.

Sis shared his unquestioning religious faith and she often joined her women neighbors before Easter in scrubbing the floors of Nativity of Our Lord Church — the Bridgeport church where the Mayor had been baptized, where he had been an altar boy, where he had married Sis and where funeral services were held for his parents. But that church the Mayor usually reserved for days off, for private and personal times.

Most weekdays he attended one of two downtown churches — Old St. Mary's, E. Van Buren and S. Wabash, or St. Peter's, 110 W. Madison. The 7:15 A.M. mass at Old St. Mary's was often his choice when something was disturbing him, when he wished to be alone. At the 7:45 A.M. St. Peter's mass he would more likely be engaged in conversation by an acquaintance, but this church was also best for getting in and out on a tightly scheduled day.

After church the Mayor went to his office and the day-to-day realities of politics and government. Being an observant Catholic was certainly no hindrance to him in Chicago. Over 1,750,000 followers of the religion made the city the

Pope Paul VI poses with Mayor and Mrs. Daley in the Pontiff's Vatican Palace studio during a private audience granted May 9, 1964 (opposite). The Daleys were on vacation in Europe.

90

largest Roman Catholic archdiocese in North America.

Despite the Mayor's devotion to his religion, he could voice his opinion strongly when he felt the Catholic leadership was out of place. When the Church fathers raised a furor concerning Presidential candidate Jimmy Carter and his position on the abortion issue, the Mayor declared: "No priest can tell the people how to vote."

When the Mayor returned home after a hard day and retired for the evening, he turned once again to his religion. At funeral services for the Mayor the Rev. Gilbert Graham, a longtime friend, recalled: "He once told me he never needed any sleeping medication because he always had the rosary, and it calmed him and prepared him for rest no matter what the problems of the day might have been."

While visiting the Vatican, the Daleys stop to admire St. Peter's Square (below).

The Mayor arrives in Milwaukee by train on November 15, 1958, to escort Archbishop Albert G. Meyer to his new post as head of Chicago's Roman Catholic Archdiocese, the largest archdiocese in the United States (above). At the Mayor's right is Dan Ryan, president of the Cook County Board of Commissioners; at his left is Milwaukee Alderman Charles Quirk.

Mayor Daley greets Archbishop Meyer at the chancery in Milwaukee (left).

Illinois Governor Otto Kerner, Mayor Daley and Mrs. Daley witness the installation of The Most Rev. John Patrick Cody as Archbishop of the Archdiocese of Chicago, August 24, 1965 (above)

Mayor Daley is interviewed at Rome Airport on June 25, 1967, as he arrives to attend the elevation to the purple of Archbishop John Cody of Chicago (left).

The Mayor was proud to express his profound religious beliefs and his love of friends and family (opposite).

A SPORTSMAN

A
Sportsman

As one of his last official acts Mayor Richard J. Daley of Chicago took a basketball shot. It was a two-hand set shot and Daley was showing some youths at a new park dedication how they did it when he was a young man with the Hamburg Athletic Club.

Daley never lost the enthusiasm for sports he developed as manager of the Hamburg teams.

"He was a very busy guy, but he took the job seriously," recalled Lawrence F. O'Neill, one of Daley's teammates in the HAC. "He made the lineups, booked the games and ran the team on the field."

Earlier, Daley had been a good quarterback, a good-field-no-hit infielder and an average-shooting guard for the Hamburg football, baseball and basketball teams.

Though as Mayor, Daley never exaggerated his own athletic prowess, he applied his energy and administrative abilities to providing facilities for Chicago's neighborhood sportsmen and keeping Chicago's professional teams healthy and in Chicago.

When it appeared that the White Sox were in danger of being bought and moved elsewhere, Daley gave Bill Veeck full support in his efforts to purchase the team and retain it for Chicago.

"He was a good friend to me and the White Sox when the going was difficult," recalled Veeck, "And that's the true test."

Daley had a meeting with Veeck after the sale seemed to stall and later persuaded his friend, Canteen Corporation president Patrick O'Malley, to invest $200,000 in the project.

Former middleweight boxing great Tony Zale, now an employee of the Chicago Park District, playfully blocks a left hook from the Mayor during dedication ceremonies of a remodeled fieldhouse, February 23, 1975 (above).

"Oh, how he liked sports," recalled O'Malley. "I bet I got called 12 times and he'd say, 'Let's go out to the game. Get a hold of Helen, I'll get Sis and we'll go out and see the White Sox.'"

Though Daley and Bears owner George Halas remained friends, they had a brief rift when Halas wanted to move the football team to Arlington Heights.

"They can move to Arlington Heights but if they do they can't call themselves the Chicago Bears," snapped Daley. "They'll be the Arlington Bears."

But of all the sports, Daley's favorite was fishing.

"He was a great fisherman, he loved fishing," recalled Pat O'Malley. "He had all the outfits and lines and he would work on those little hooks by himself."

"It's the one place where you're closest to God," said Daley.

On the last day of his life, there was some concern that Daley might embarrass himself on the basketball court in that little neighborhood park.

His younger companions missed their shots.

Dick Daley made his.

Mayor Daley presents the Grantland Rice Award to Chicago Daily News sports editor John Carmichael during a luncheon at the Hotel Astor in New York, November 1, 1963 (above). Beaming her approval at center is Mrs. Carmichael.

The Mayor prepares to hurl the proverbial "first ball" before the 1976 baseball season opener between the Chicago White Sox and the Kansas City Royals in Chicago, April 9. White Sox president Bill Veeck, at the Mayor's right, gets out of the way of the throw (above).

White Sox batboy Dave Sortal gets a ball autographed by the number-one Sox fan, Richard J. Daley, before the White Sox-Cubs annual charity game, June 24, 1971 (below). (The Sox won, 7 - 3.)

Baseball games were often family events for the Daleys (above).

Mayor Daley makes his last official appearance, dedicating an addition to a fieldhouse at Mann Park on Chicago's South Side (above). At the Mayor's left is Peter K. Klein, Chicago Park District assistant director of recreation; Walter Lis, dressed as Santa Claus; and 10th Ward Ald. Edward Vrdolyak, shooting a basket.

104

Dick Daley makes his shot on the basketball court at Mann Park, December 20, 1976 (below).

THE
END
CAME
QUICKLY

The End Came Quickly

Another typically busy day in the life of Mayor Richard J. Daley was his last. The only thing unusual about the morning was Sis Daley accompanied her husband downtown. They hosted the Mayor's annual Christmas breakfast for city officials.

The breakfast was held in the Medill Room of the Bismarck Hotel. While the happy gathering ate eggs Benedict, bacon, sausage and sweet rolls and drank Irish coffee, a Chicago Symphony harpist played Christmas carols and Irish songs, including the Mayor's favorite, *Danny Boy*. When the meal was over, the Mayor was presented with a pair of round-trip tickets to Ireland. They had been donated by the city's department heads.

"From our home to your home," said the Mayor, visibly moved, "we wish you one thing — good health, happiness and a very Merry Christmas."

After the breakfast, the Mayor left the hotel and walked across the street to City Hall. He took the elevator to the fifth floor and spent the rest of the morning in his office.

The Mayor was soon visited by sculptress Eleanor Root. She presented him with busts of himself and Sis and said, "You're the most wonderful and best mayor in the world."

Shortly before noon the Mayor took the elevator to the lobby and strode out into the street. He noticed workers and artists creating big, beautiful ice sculptures in the Civic Center Plaza, across from the Picasso statue, and he walked over and watched them for a while. Then he got into his limousine.

The car moved away from the curb and, sometime during the ride, Daley

Anxious passersby wait for news of the Mayor's condition as Richard M. Daley, still in casual clothing, arrives at 900 N. Michigan (above).

made a startling remark to his bodyguard: he had had a pain across his chest that morning; would the bodyguard call Dr. Thomas Coogan, Jr., his personal physician, and make an appointment for that afternoon.

First, though, the Mayor had a commitment to dedicate a new $545,000 gymnasium at Mann Park, 130th Street and South Carondolet Avenue, about 12:30 P.M.

"This building is dedicated to the people of this great community," the Mayor told the 250 persons gathered. "They are making Chicago a better city, because when you have a good neighborhood, you have a good city, and this is a good neighborhood."

Then it was on to the North Side, to 900 North Michigan, for an examination by Dr. Coogan. The doctor gave the Mayor an electrocardiogram which detected an irregular heartbeat. The Mayor spoke to his son Michael on the phone, and it was decided the Mayor would enter nearby Northwestern Memorial Hospital.

While the doctor was in another room, phoning the hospital, he heard the Mayor fall. He rushed back into the examining room and found him lying on the

Heather Morgan, head of Chicago's fine arts department, and Lewis Hill, commissioner of development and planning, rush to the Mayor's office upon hearing the news that Mayor Daley has been stricken.

Tragedy befell the Mayor's family in 1974, when he collapsed with what was later determined to be a major stroke. Here, daughter Mary Carol Vanecko, accompanied by a plainclothes policeman, races to the entrance of Rush-Presbyterian-St. Luke's Hospital, May 7, 1974 (opposite).

Crowds gather, blocking traffic on Michigan Avenue and surrounding streets, while medical personnel work to try to revive the Mayor (above).

Policemen watch, sadly, as the Fire Department ambulance, carrying the body of Mayor Daley, arrives at the McKeon Funeral Home, 634 W. 37th St. (below).

floor. After calling for aid, he knelt and gave the Mayor mouth-to-mouth resuscitation.

Minutes later, three paramedics from Fire Department Ambulance 42 took over. They were relieved by doctors who arrived one by one from the Wesley Pavilion of Northwestern Memorial Hospital.

Every medical approach was tried and discarded as the Mayor's family — four sons, three daughters and his wife — arrived and dropped to their knees in prayer.

At 3:50 P.M., the end was officially declared.

The ambulance was brought to the rear of the building, the Mayor's body put in and, with six squad cars as escort the vehicle headed for the South Side, to the McKeon Funeral Home.

Sis Daley would later tell Judge Abraham Lincoln Marovitz, a family intimate, that she was glad that her husband had gone quickly with no pain.

Bridgeport was quiet that night.

"We cry for our friend, we cry for our neighbor," said Rev. John Lydon, the Daleys' pastor. "But Richard Daley wouldn't want us to spend a lot of time crying."

THE CITY WITH THE BIG SHOULDERS MOURNS

The City With The Big Shoulders Mourns

It was 7 A.M. Wednesday morning when Senator Richard M. Daley shook hands with the last of the mourners, the last of a line of some 100,000 who had paid their final respects to Richard's father since noon Tuesday. Richard stood in the nave of Nativity of Our Lord Church, a simple, white brick church on the South Side where Mayor Richard J. Daley had worshipped most of his life, where he had married Eleanor "Sis" Guilfoyle. Mayor Daley now lay in state as his good people of Chicago bid him farewell and his son shook their hands.

The night before, the Mayor's entire family had greeted mourners, six of the seven children shaking hands. Daughter Mary Carol sat with her mother Sis near the coffin.

The mayor lay in a white-lined, mahogany coffin, attired in a blue suit, a white shirt and a blue tie, a rosary in his hands. A policeman passed out a small card to each mourner who filed past. The card was imprinted with a picture of the Mayor smiling on the front and the Mayor's favorite prayer, that of St. Francis of Assisi, on the back.

Some mourners had cleared the aisle Tuesday night so that members of the Shannon Rovers Pipers Band could play *Garryowen*. This was at the request of Sis Daley, who said it was one of her husband's favorites.

It had been planned to close the church at 10 P.M. Tuesday night, but the line of mourners appeared never-ending. Even as the temperature dropped to 10 degrees, the Ninth District police commander announced: "As long as there's anyone waiting to get in, we will not turn anyone away."

Even when the church was supposed to close for a security check at 5 A.M. Wednesday, Richard M. Daley ordered that the doors stay open.

116

In the bitter Chicago cold, over 100,000 people came to view Mayor Daley's body lying in state at Nativity of Our Lord Church (above).

At 9:30 A.M. Wednesday a requiem mass was offered. Most of the 1,000 seats in the church were taken by influential people, including President-elect Jimmy Carter, Vice-President Nelson Rockefeller and Senator Ted Kennedy. The streets were filled with people who didn't have enough clout to merit a precious entrance ticket. They heard the services through mounted loudspeakers.

Rev. Gilbert Graham, a lifelong friend of the mayor, told the assemblage: "Mrs. Daley asked that there be no formal eulogy. It wasn't his style. The quality of his life and actions are enough eulogy." Rev. Graham also said that the mayor had been paid a moving tribute by the thousands of working-class people who had gathered throughout the long bitterly cold night.

John Cardinal Cody concluded the service by reading a wire from the Vatican Secretary of State that conveyed the blessings of Pope Paul VI. A solo by Lyric Opera tenor Frank Little accompanied the distribution of communion.

As the Mayor's coffin was carried from the church, it was blessed by Cardinal Cody before being placed in the hearse. Policemen and firemen formed an honor guard.

Mrs. Daley and other family members rode to the cemetery in the Mayor's

Mourners enter and leave Nativity of Our Lord Church (above).

John Cardinal Cody (above), archbishop of the Archdiocese of Chicago, conducted Mayor Daley's funeral mass.

Chicago police and firemen salute the coffin of Mayor Daley as it is taken into the church (right).

Three of Mayor Daley's children, Eleanor (left), Patricia and Richard M., leave the church to enter the limousine that will take them to Holy Sepulchre Cemetery (above).

Mayor Daley's son Richard, his wife Sis and his daughter Eleanor leave the church following the funeral mass on Wednesday, December 22 (right).

Among the many dignitaries attending the Mayor's funeral were (from left) President-elect Jimmy Carter, columnist Ann Landers, Senator Edward M. Kennedy (D.-Mass.) and Vice-President Nelson Rockefeller (opposite).

The last of the mourners leave Nativity of Our Lord Church after the funeral (above).

Mayor Daley's admirers from all walks of life,
from near and far, came to pay their last respects
(right).

A woman weeps near Mayor Daley's coffin (above).

Mayor Daley's widow, on the arm of her son, State Sen. Richard M. Daley, leaves her husband's gravesite at Holy Sepulchre Cemetery. At Mrs. Daley's left is her daughter, Eleanor (right).

The gravesite of Mayor Daley is near the graves of his father and mother, Michael and Lillian Daley (left).

Thousands of people watch as the funeral procession enters Holy Sepulchre Cemetery in suburban Worth (opposite).

The main entrance of the Old Board of Health Building, 54 West Hubbard Street, is draped in black in mourning for Mayor Daley (below).

Among the many floral tributes was this one sent by the Chicago Police Department (left).

Billboards and signs throughout the city spoke a fond farewell to Chicago's Mayor (right).

Chicago City Council members eulogize the Mayor in a memorial service held in Council chambers on December 27 (above).

Mayor Daley addressed the Chicago City Council from this chair for over 21 years (opposite).

128

limousine, pausing in front of their South Lowe Avenue bungalow. Several thousand mourners walked alongside.

Brief graveside rites were privately held at the Holy Sepulchre Cemetery, Worth, Illinois, and the Mayor was laid to rest in the Daley plot near the grave of his mother, Lillian, and his father, Michael. Some 3,000 people gathered outside the cemetery.

The following Monday, in the City Council chambers, Chicago said its official goodbye to Richard J. Daley. The black-and-purple-draped chambers held more than 600 persons. Some of the city's alderman spoke for all of them in paying their final respects to Daley. Representing the Daley family were the Mayor's four sons, William, Richard M., John Patrick, and Michael, and his son-in-law, Dr. Robert Vanecko.

An invocation was offered by John Cardinal Cody which praised the Mayor as "a man whose best monument will be a city that continues to work, where all families find opportunity, justice and love."

Richard M. Daley gave a statement which said, in part: "My mother and our family gratefully acknowledge the many kind and thoughtful expressions of sympathy and especially the prayers of so many at this time."

But perhaps the most fitting remark concerning Richard J. Daley's death had been made by the Mayor himself on his 70th birthday. A City Hall secretary had said that Richard J. Daley would always be Mayor of Chicago, and the Mayor replied, "The future belongs to the Lord himself. Where I go, and how long I am able to serve the people of Chicago, depends on Him.

REFLECTIONS

Pope Paul VI

Vatican City

[*Taken from a wire from the Vatican Secretary of State to John Cardinal Cody.*] The Holy Father received your message notifying him of the sudden death of Mayor Richard Daley. On this sad occasion, he offers expression of his paternal sympathy to Mrs. Daley and her family to whom he also imparts his apostolic blessing and pledge of comfort and Christian hope. His Holiness gives the assurance of his prayers for Mayor Daley, invoking for him eternal rest in the peace of the risen Christ.

132

John Cardinal Cody

Archdiocese of Chicago

We know that the spirit of Richard J. Daley will live on, not only here but on the city blocks. We were privileged to have a leader who could only be described as great. He was in touch with the people, smiling in their joy, weeping in their sorrow. In this instance, words of praise fail.

Jimmy Carter

President of the United States

He was a great and good friend to me and a great Democratic leader. He led his city of Chicago, always with the best interest of its people at heart. He had their trust and administered their affairs in an exemplary manner. He was a good man, a man who loved his family and the people of Chicago. He will be missed. Mayor Daley was a good man and, I thought, a superb mayor. When I began my political campaign several years ago, most of the influential political leaders paid very little attention to me. But he was always interested in me and gave me encouragement. I never had any difficulty at all getting him on the telephone, and he gave me good advice. I considered him to be one of my personal friends.

Gerald Ford

Former President of the United States

Mayor Daley has been a dominant force in American politics for many years. His career of public service at the state and city level, and his participation in national legislation and policies reflect his strong belief in and dedication to the vitality of the American cities. Though controversial at times, he has been a towering figure in the American scene and will be long remembered by the people of Chicago, of Illinois and of the nation.

133

George C. Wallace

Governor, State of Alabama

I knew the warm, tender side of him expressed in a telephone call when I was sick in Maryland. He said, "Keep your chin up. Mrs. Daley and I pray for you every day, and we know you're going to get well." This was a side of Mayor Daley that many people did not know.

Edward Kennedy

U.S. Senator, Massachusetts

Richard Daley will be remembered as one of America's greatest mayors, a leader who understood the needs and aspirations of his city, who made Chicago livable, who kept his city as a beacon of wise and responsible leadership for every other major city in this nation.

ames R. Thompson
overnor, State of Illinois

part of Chicago died with the passing of Mayor aley. I am saddened by his death. We will miss im — he was a great mayor, a fact not always nderstood by his critics, but one over-helmingly confirmed by the citizens of hicago.

Dan Walker
Former Governor, State of Illinois

Mayor Daley was as much an institution of Chicago as the office he held. His accomplishments for the city he loved will long be remembered. His devotion to Chicago and the Democratic party was exceeded only by his deep love for his family. His influence was felt around the nation. He was as much at home dining with presidents in the White House as he was eating hot dogs in Comiskey Park, cheering the White Sox.

135

Adlai Stevenson III
U.S. Senator, Illinois

He worked, rising at dawn each day, to serve the
public, his party, and his family. That was his
life. He was as unselfish a man as I have ever
known. The public has lost a rare public servant,
and I have lost a friend.

Charles R. Perc
U.S. Senator, Illinoi

He was a fiercely partisan Democrat, but he wa
utterly fair and courteous to those who oppose
him, and he was completely nonpartisan i
building a better and greater Chicago.

136

oman Pucinski

1st Ward Alderman, City of Chicago

e forgot how to say no. Every time someone anted him for an event, he was so consenting bout it — it was as if he were trying to telescope s much as possible of his life in as short a time s possible. I get the feeling he had a premonion and wanted to do as much good for people as e could. Even in his heyday, he didn't have as eavy a schedule. The poor guy just worked imself to death.

George W. Dunne

President, Cook County Board of Commissioners; Chairman, Cook County Democratic Party Central Committee

The city of Chicago has lost its greatest booster and supporter, and Richard J. Daley has died in the service of the people of Chicago. That is the way he would want to go, because he loved this city so much. Mayor Daley lived for Chicago. The mayor loved Chicago, and, in effect, he died for Chicago. Almighty God must have loved all of us. The entire city of Chicago is a memorial.

137

J. Terrence Brunner

Executive Director, Better Government Association

Although the BGA frequently disagreed with the mayor over matters of policy, Mayor Daley consistently showed himself to be a man of compassion who worked tirelessly to improve the lives of all Chicago's citizens. Mayor Daley made a significant and enduring contribution to this city and his leadership will be sorely missed.

William A. Singer

Attorney; Former 43rd Ward Alderman, City of Chicago

Mayor Daley was Chicago. He was a part of every one of us. Although I was his opponent, I have great respect for him as a man and for his extraordinary accomplishments. Like millions of others, I am saddened by his loss.

Leon M. Despres

Attorney; Former 5th Ward Alderman, City of Chicago

He was the ablest party chairman that the Democratic Party has had in its history, the strongest mayor the city had in its history. I liked him personally. What he did was right as he saw it.

ev. Jesse Jackson

ational President, Operation PUSH

epresented what I call the loyal opposition on
any occasions, but with a profound sense of
spect. The mayor, history will record, was a
emier mayor.

Ralph H. Metcalfe

Representative, First Congressional
District, Illinois

The world will little note, nor long remember
what we say here, but it can never forget what
we did here.

Patrick O'Malley
Chairman, Canteen Corporation

He was a great fellow. The man had a great
sense of humor. He had a laugh that was con-
tagious. When you were alone with him, he'd get
serious and talk about his family, his church, the
City of Chicago. I know I'm going to lose some of
my enthusiasm because he isn't going to be there
to talk about it, to banter back and forth on
issues.

Michael J. Howle
Former Secretary of Stat
State of Illino

In the character of his private life, as a husbar
and a father, as well as in all other aspects of h
life he was a model to all who knew him. It w
an honor to be numbered among his friends.

aron Gold

Columnist, *Chicago Tribune*

loved him. There were a lot of things he did wrong — but everyone does things wrong. And he d so many things right that his few mistakes dn't matter. Here's an example of how much aley loved Chicago. When Queen Elizabeth II sited the city, Daley was showing her around. hile on the tour Daley was heard to comment, he's so pretty!'' Everyone assumed he was re rring to the Queen, but someone asked him yway.

"I mean the City of Chicago!" was Daley's im ediate response.

Maggie Daly

Columnist, *Chicago Tribune*

In all the years I knew the mayor, I somehow felt that no matter what was wrong, he could make it right because of his strength and his honor. When I heard the tragic news, somehow the Christmas lights seemed to become dimmer and the Christmas carols seemed to lose their joy . . . and all I know at this moment . . . is I feel an emptiness of the soul.

George Halas

Chairman of the Board, Chicago Bears

Dick Daley was the mayor of Chicago but he was really the father of Chicago. He loved Chicago with a father's love. I lost a great friend. Chicago lost a great leader.

Bill Veec

President, Chicago White Sc

I feel that personally, I have lost a great frien The city has lost a great friend too. I feel May Daley was irreplaceable. There were times wh we did not agree, philosophically, but I alwa admired him. I truly think he kept the city goir singlehandedly.

Frank Sinatra

Entertainer

He was a fine official and he was a good friend to me. I will miss him, and Chicago will never be the same.

Bob Hope
Entertainer

His service to the people of the Chicago area has been an inspiration to all mayors and people everywhere. Chicago is a model for the whole country, he was able to keep his city humming. He will be missed.

143

Richard J. Daley 1902-1976

May the road rise up to meet you,
may the wind be at your back,
and may God hold you in the palm of His hand.